Anaphora

poems by

Joddy Murray

Finishing Line Press
Georgetown, Kentucky

Anaphora

Copyright © 2020 by Joddy Murray
ISBN 978-1-64662-171-2 First Edition
All rights reserved under International and Pan-American Copyright Conventions. No part of this book may be reproduced in any manner whatsoever without written permission from the publisher, except in the case of brief quotations embodied in critical articles and reviews.

ACKNOWLEDGMENTS

I am grateful to Kathleen Peirce for her poetry, mentorship, friendship, and her close reading of early drafts of these poems. I would not be the poet I am today without her influence. I dedicate these poems to my magnificent partner in life, Cisalee, who inspires me and who is the source of whatever I've come to know about love.

Publisher: Leah Maines
Editor: Christen Kincaid
Cover Art: Joddy Murray
Author Photo: Cisalee Morris
Cover Design: Elizabeth Maines McCleavy

Printed in the USA on acid-free paper.
Order online: www.finishinglinepress.com
also available on amazon.com

Author inquiries and mail orders:
Finishing Line Press
P. O. Box 1626
Georgetown, Kentucky 40324
U. S. A.

Table of Contents

My desire / pleases you 1
None think / night is / empty 2
There are / bodies 3
Days are / children 4
In the / bright day 5
We seek / nothing 6
Five snails / cooking 7
Moments / for business 8
I lust 9
I fear 10
Iron melts / reluctantly 11
O, cardinal 12
Even snakes / bathe 13
My demands 14
Grapefruit 15
This leaky / ground 16
The heart 17
Pleasure— 18
Tonight 19
No more / unhappy stars 20
Unlike the moon 21
Light grows 22
A gecko 23
I try 24
Rings in / a line 25
Come 26
Trances here 27
No possibilities 28
Going back / before habit 29
To stand / sweating 30
Take me 31
Glassblowers 32
I beckon / no one 33
I sit / empty 34
Before you / fall 35
I called / to mountains 36

My desire
pleases you,
I think.
It must.
You wake
near me
and laugh.

The day you bought me cymbidiums, they
bloomed continuously all winter—I've counted
twenty-five already. How is that possible? I
think of nothing but how lonely they are to advertise
so much of themselves. Each day I water them, trim
their leaves, and dream about their perfect bodies.
Sounds lovers repeat themselves are like these petals,
but what makes each one so distinguished in its
solitude? You come to me and smell my showered
back. I hear. Hairs on my skin cry out and rise.

None think
night is
empty—that
only insects
repeat songs
and anxieties
through loss.

Truth is, curtains over earth have holes
in them—brightness is everywhere. What is it
you would take across the strobe of space?
Elders take nothing, and they hear rivers tuned
to the same frequency as the sun. You would
do well to think what thrives in the night,
under the multi-eyed stare of heaven.
Would you carry such a heavy body so far every
night? I could stand completely still as you
wipe your answers across my lips with honey.

There are
bodies I
long to
touch, to
kiss, that
exist only
with you.

My shape is rounder now, slower.
There was a time you would awaken late
with me, open all the doors and windows
in the house, and let me feed you the arching
flesh that clung in ovals onto mango seeds.
Those were the days for bodies. Yesterday,
while you cleaned the table, I put my head
on your shoulder and felt that same numbing
breeze. It was saying something to me about
distances and our own celestial, heaving spin.

Days are
children.
I think
nobody plays
so cruelly
with innocent,
beautiful creatures.

To insist on creating again and again,
to chant and recite, to open wound after wound,
eternally, must prove how desperate we are.
Parents, no matter how benevolent, slip in air,
turn their tears to rain, flood revenge over hands,
dump their waste heavily like clay. I cannot
look up when the peril is surrounding my feet,
my shadow. Forgiveness, like surgery, is not love
or grace. I am my own tensed cheek muscle,
my own balled fist raised and hot.

In the
bright day
I imagine
your feet
are cool
and resting
in sand.

This small locket contains your weighty
hair coiled, thick with grease. There are
days I look at it, frightened. How could
it ever be enough to open such a small thing?
Nothing I lock away will compete with the pull,
the bloom of your eyes in the morning. If I
had a magic shadow, one I could trick into
following directions, I would tuck it deep
into the hidden dent at the top of your head:
a place I discovered before you did.

We seek
nothing
and know
how a mind
splits under
the weight
of itself.

As we work, we are reminded again
why this world spins so solidly
with its dusty satellite—why we must
refill our lives from time to time.
Some crane their own neck for the ax,
and during the worst days, so do we.
Eyes do not wait for what they can see.
We rely on our tongue and its juicy
memory for that. The stove creaks with
the strain of heat on its triumphant skin.

Five snails
cooking in
butter. You
with wine,
me with
goats-milk
and cheese.

This is the time when the heat outside
flashed everything into a blue quiet—
songbirds sleep, the cat yawns. Food
must be as light as the buzz of your snore,
as delicious as your wet skin. Nothing
blooms. Down the street, there is music.
I have made my peace with love, and,
so far, you silently argue it. I want
to bathe you, push water through
your hair, make room for light. Praise.

Moments
for business
are painful.
I see you
aging every
summer
before me.

There are wrinkles in all things. I don't
notice them all the time, they're so common.
The tortoise hinges her neck on them,
encasing and revealing them at will. Your neck
is haltingly smooth and, too many times,
tempting. In those moments that stretch
forever, I seek you out, sneak-up like a cat,
and with the ax of my lips, taste the curve
like a train tastes the rail—a gliding
that both is and is not the line of you.

I lust
because
emptiness
is not
optional,
not the
quiet end.

Gases and lavas and excited atoms
all know a chaos like I know this window,
its frame neatly tucked inside rubbery insulation.
Mirrors, once fooled but never again, know
this lust too, just as they know themselves.
What I know about seeing you taught me through
hope, curiosity, and the way you keep egg cartons
balanced by arranging for the missing eggs inside.
What is it you want to say to me, my eager
mouth in yours, our lips sore and wet?

I fear
floods. How
much water
can rise
with each
pass of
our satellite?

Today, when you wept, you bent your eyes
to each of their corners to prevent me from
comforting you—but only for so long. Ice
cream whites dome each pupil, and as blood
pinkens, I know enough by now to listen
and roll with you. Then what I really hear
is a small aching replay within myself as if my
own ribs press in to ask *How long now before
I set my own iron doors free to see you blurred
as you see me? Who is this waiting in me?*

Iron melts
reluctantly.
Deep inside,
purity toughens,
pulls length
into an alloyed
whole, impure.

True, the sun is no match for the cold
space around it just as I am no match
for the sun. In space, my body becomes
just another moon, half-frozen, orbiting
without choice. My plumage in front
is bedazzled with ice. Every pass toward
you is just a year for me. I remind you
how blind this little blue planet can be,
its own moon parting with a shiver and a nod
as I part its path, stubborn and singing alone.

O, cardinal,
soldier of
every pole,
what gift
is better
than that
red badge?

My red flows within. It's so common
that few—oysters, milkweed—do not
share it. But you stand poised, still.
Your perch is pressed oil and cables
that link themselves together so when
you call out, she will hear. Unlike you, my badge—
its internal, scarlet wanderings—is common enough.
As you call out to your mate on another pole,
do not think so much of yourself or your clarity.
You and I, we exchange in hearty, cracked longing.

Even snakes
bathe. They
sense how
undervalued
the privilege
and release
from gravity

is. Because what is before and after is only
known by one name: blood. What
you stop for is not your pleasure.
Winds and tides and drippy heavens
do not substitute. As surely as they
remain adamant, so do I. The
brainy fire that spews is molten
happiness is madness—a rock's bath.
Watch the dragonfly. See the joy there?
Stop under the waterfall and feel its urgency.

My demands
are simple:
you must
press, two-
handed, on
my chest
until I exhale.

A black crane lifts off, alone, and
mussels give to their boiling broth
all they can. You have time to laugh—
your body, lit and flowered, a thickened
tea for drinking. These vocal chords
weaken my resolve for silence and
tepid, fatty foods. I have come
to lift your desire. To have you push me
this way joins us. Centers collapse
and what is left rubs gloriously together.

Grapefruit,
four in
a bowl,
open to
you, pink
and sweet.
I watch.

Your ritual includes the usual circum-
navigated cut, no sugar, a spoon balanced
between fingers you lick often. Dismayed,
I salivate for what I've never liked and you,
contented, will still bend each half into a spout
and squeeze the juices down. I've been caught
there and made to fight back out of your mouth.
It's not easy. The danger is being stuck under
longing, its burs and juices drowning me.
There are times you are just too warm to leave.

This leaky
ground still
will hold
pools up.
It suppurates
under each
fallen death.

As old as it is, it knows its caves,
its ice, all of its buried and living.
Heat and cold are not opposites.
In this ground, the grandmother
of every synapse, every connected branch,
is the sound of the first day ringing on and on.
Do you hear? How far will I dig to reveal
this tremor? I may walk above this skin, but
more water than dust fills and falls and
moves my body into sleek and foreign air.

The heart
when allowed,
will only
cover itself,
scar. You
pull me
over you.

Where are your eyes now? I stopped
searching once. The sun and its solipsistic
family finished their mirage—their trickery
set in waves that circulate, crazed. Did you release
another set of hopes as you searched for
me in your blindness? I'll put this garland
of rose petal, a sheet of stitched vine, some
almonds, and a shirt ripped from my chest
on the doorstep for you—but hurry.
Thieves here treasure any offering.

Pleasure—
listen my
garden—
is the
bee that
touches
each prize.

It is not a construct. It lives. It moves
from place to place because overexposure
kills passion. To take such a thing and hold
on to it is not new or frightening—at least
not as much as it is maddening fruit, ripening.
Forests and stars know to fear what we do not.
Recognize, my garden, and stay a while
for the drunken bee as it touches each adulterated
petal, each new leaf that is barely open,
yet chewed—there may be no reason to escape.

Tonight
I'm sure
the night's
pale dolor
will feed.
In hunger,
hunger endures.

Your hips rise for me and, in that dimension,
there is no time for hesitancy—
the dead speak of this. Together, we know
this rage is as temporal as appetite, as
reoccurring. My fingers carve your outline
like a sentry, my hands redder and plump.
Hairs tangle, mix. Afterwards, as you
cradle into me and sleep comes, my
nakedness becomes your nakedness—our
generous howling in each slowing breath.

No more
unhappy stars
should pass
over these
lovers tonight.
The moon
shadows them.

Together, holding each other tightly,
summer shimmies itself over our bodies
like fat. Each stage before and after we eat
dinner builds our anticipation for the next
spotlight, the next reflected crier from space.
Why do we keep arriving in rain and snow
with bad bread and cheese we never can
identify in the dark, or in busy traffic?
We must not know anything about the shapes
under rocks that look up only to behold.

Unlike the
moon, my
task quietly
completes as
I wear
down: a
hurried glimmer.

The sun willfully tasks me. My face,
sun-burned tired, fades like house paint.
Across the ocean you rest on the ground
describing the carpet, windows, plants.
I've seen rain for days. Now, asking
you about love, the clouds drag and roll
themselves towards you. The young elm outside
warns me—*Don't give it all away! Keep
yourself some small thing.* You lift from bed
slowly: shadow remains. You lift summer.

Light grows
as day
convinces us
to sleep,
exposed here,
nude, in
landscapes.

Flooded by gifts of fruit, my appreciation tires.
Candles, fragrances, the seeded quarter of
an apple—I trust only the small things in a lie,
the rising tones and falling eyelids. Your
speed, the sheepish crawl of a stink bug near you,
makes you seem lovelier just as years are lovely.
I cherish the tawdry dryer, the spongy washer.
We launder together and spark cloudy days into
flashes as durable as smiles. Such a collection,
even incomplete, keeps winds crouched at the door.

A gecko
attempts warmth.
I listen
for peaceful
or leggy
shadows walled
with me.

Approval takes its form as desire. We
sit with our hands drunk on lemon, tea.
There is silence under your eyes, in rings,
that shakes itself in thunder as perspiration
races to the bottom of our glasses. You nod.
I dip my fingers in that, like I would with any star,
and swirl them around—a heavy fire-nugget
perfect for giving—even dead lovers erected
in their stony chambers will recognize with muddy,
iridescent glances how far my arms reach for you.

I try
not to
tell you
my dreams.
They are
colorless
half-truths.

In one, you drowned. I swam
with the flood as it washed us, together,
into drumming falls and branches. We
managed to stay connected, by waist or hand,
in the heaped waters. But then you went under
and breathed—the awful end of you. I tried
to follow you to the land of the dead, but your
spirit wanted nothing of my rubbery skin.
I tried to kiss you. There was fire,
some yelling. In time, you forgot me.

Rings in
a line
form one
thousand eyes
and faces:
hundreds of
tensile sanities.

Like the comet, I have forged myself into
hoops of similarity, made myself longer
and scented. Never before has this body
known such slender, airy shapes. I make
my own clamor; I sink slower in water. The
slipping wind whistles past my empty groin.
For a metal, life grows busier with clamor—
I keep things down, apart, up. Where there
is weakness, I collapse and convolute
inside touch. What you see is skin.

Come. Let
me rub
oil on
you to
soothe us
both through
this heat.

Our day clicks past; insects crawl to nap.
Am I causing this? Rub my back. Iron
the tendons and mounds that resist
under your hands that know the sacred
is unsaid. You keep saying how these
blue pressures corroborate to find
us under watery sheets stained with
our defenses, our honeyed sweat.
I can't sleep until you have thought of
everything we forget to celebrate each hour.

Trances here
are common.
Discarded
prophets
pace, looking
for faith
anywhere.

The unloved are looking also and I don't
know how they can stay warm and relaxed.
I won't waste days as clouds waste time
looking for one another, repeating paths
at the whim of the wind. I scratch;
somewhere on the planet another itch shows
up, quickly reddened by nails as long as a gust
and tempered only by subtle decay and attention.
I understand how absolute and meaty
the arrangement is—love and pain, together.

No possibilities,
only the
swift action
of clouds—
hurricanes that
re-root trees
miles away.

Permanence. The hardest thing is not
finding desire or keeping it. It's the variety
in ant colonies, the flight of a cicada,
the heavy path of freezing rain. You
may sit and watch, but to be here
you must find a space in laughter:
experience texture without touch
or the sloppy pull of a hook in your mouth.
Today's weather changes, then drags the same
noiseless violence through scattered stems.

Going back
before habit,
when one
pulse drowns
another, fan-
tailed crimson
brilliances

fly outside as I taste bread for the first time.
Back to the beginning—when souls shake
winds aside like trees do, littering their feet
with fruit—I've come to receive a small
present, timeless and unencumbered.
It's not just hard to accept you, hard
to imagine your love for me, but also, like
now, there is the crackle of your saliva,
the fragrance of your salty tears. I am
tucked within you, as in an envelope, sealed.

To stand
sweating, alone,
on a rock
before you,
for you,
is tender
and stupid.

What we do in such places is meet our belonging
like the sand meets itself, as stranger
of itself, carved of itself, lasting, minute.
I place petals from my pockets on your dark
eyelashes and in this stillness no wind moves
them. You throw off your dress, run to the sea,
and disappear like a minnow, blind from its
own chrome-plated skin. I know you swim
well, that the sand has a thousand eyes, but
in case the ocean loves its guests, I follow.

Take me
into our home.
Slip my
head into
cool water.
Do this
when I die.

Don't let me lay in the garden, or
over the table, or stooped by the bed. Dry
my bones in the oven (don't forget
to take out the skillets) and take care
to wash yourself of any opportunistic,
yet vital, parasites that will hang on,
as I did. Pull away from me anything
that will remain, and bake at 400 degrees,
or until my hands look as though your
supple kiss scented them with fine carbon.

Glassblowers
know how
stars are
made. Color
added last
stubbornly bonds
fire to fire.

Many stars are latecomers—they've
been sending us messages you and I
do not distinguish from our humming.
As each dotted spirit seems to run
directly into our gaze, you look to
the low horizon, before dusk, to see
which comes first in the night. *What
is this one? Venus?* The planets
fool us every time. Where am I
that these stars blast right through me?

I beckon
no one,
but come
and set
down gifts
piled on
your back.

One man with a sunburn like a rose did not know
the balms and herbs he walked on could heal it. I
have learned to talk to creatures that must always
know where I am from, or where I live, just as they
say it is clear why women live longer than men—
that there is a natural call I do not hear. In the canoe
that rocks and billows, the one by the genuflecting reeds,
spirits with salty hair argue—which one will catch
the wind, which will stay seated with the arrogant oarsman?
Below, reflections in water quickly hide themselves.

I sit
empty of
hate. Snow
outside
falls like
lashes. Fire
beats in.

I have known who will destroy me
for a while now. There is thirst and
satisfaction in each breath, each drink
of water. I choose to cradle the silence
like a lover until nobody can stop the
day's good work. There will be a day
when toothless songs echo, when I'm
neither alone or comfortable. Let it come.
Bring with it reasons packed on your head
like the ever-present lump of cooling, piled hair.

Before you
fall this
time let
me cast
a shadow
for your
lambent eyes.

The sun wants influence into the coldest
places and masked deeds. No anger,
but honest generosity as protons
leap from rock to rock in a dusty space.
Lover, as you lay down to nap I will
cup some resistance for you—let it spill
away so you can hear the gulls and
the fierce crashes of deepening waves.
I am here with you to remind myself
to remain open like the sun and give.

I called
to mountains
during the
winter melt.
They said
wait, we're
busy laughing.

The valleys flooded, and as the banks
smiled wider and wider, the fishes
all knew what to do: feed wildly the
newly drowned—feast on spring.
I boxed some jasmine for a lover,
gave it dirt and water during the journey,
but after days of descending, where
the air thickens like lava, all that was
left was the box, its scent, and my
windblown ears radiant with burns.

www.ingramcontent.com/pod-product-compliance
Lightning Source LLC
LaVergne TN
LVHW041551070426
835507LV00011B/1045